3 1288 01505 9813

MW00965754

BEING HEALTHY
Milk and Alternatives

Heather C. Hudak

Weigl

CALGARY
www.weigl.com

Published by Weigl Educational Publishers Limited
6325 10 Street S.E.
Calgary, Alberta, Canada
T2H 2Z9

Website: www.weigl.com

Copyright ©2009 Weigl Educational Publishers Limited
All rights reserved. No part of this publication may be reproduced, stored in a retrieval
system, or transmitted in any form or by any means, electronic, mechanical,
photocopying, recording, or otherwise, without the prior written permission of
the publisher.

All of the Internet URLs given in the book were valid at the time of publication. However,
due to the dynamic nature of the Internet, some addresses may have changed, or sites may
have ceased to exist since publication. While the author and publisher regret any
inconvenience this may cause readers, no responsibility for any such changes can be
accepted by either the author or the publisher.

Library and Archives Canada Cataloguing in Publication data available upon request.
Fax (403) 233-7769 for the attention of the Publishing Records department.

ISBN 978-1-55388-420-0 (hard cover)
ISBN 978-1-55388-421-7 (soft cover)

Printed in the United States of America
1 2 3 4 5 6 7 8 9 0 12 11 10 09 08

Editor: Heather C. Hudak
Design: Kathryn Livingstone, Terry Paulhus

Every reasonable effort has been made to trace ownership and to obtain
permission to reprint copyright material. The publishers would be pleased
to have any errors or omissions brought to their attention so that they may
be corrected in subsequent printings.

We gratefully acknowledge the financial support of the Government of Canada
through the Book Publishing Industry Development Program (BPIDP) for our
publishing activities.

Contents

You Are What You Eat

Fruit & Vegetables
5–6 servings

Meat & Alternatives
1–2 servings

From the top of your head to the tip of your toes, you are what you eat. To keep everything working in top form, it is important to eat a balanced diet, drink plenty of water, and be active.

How do you decide what foods to eat? Do you have a special diet, or do you eat whatever you like? There are many guides, such as Canada's Food Guide, that can help you make good choices about the foods you eat.

According to Canada's Food Guide, there are four main food groups. Eating a certain number of servings from each of the food groups every day is one way to help keep your body fit. Healthy eating habits can help prevent heart disease, **obesity**, **diabetes**, and certain types of cancers.

Canadian Food Guide
Recommended Daily Servings for Ages 4–13

Milk & Alternatives
2–4 servings

Grain Products
4–6 servings

Food for Thought

Think about the foods you ate today. How do your eating habits compare to those of other people?

Only 50 percent of Canadian children aged 4 to 18 eat the minimum recommended servings of fruit and vegetables each day.

Thirty percent of Canadian children have at least one soft drink each day.

About 75 percent of children in Canada do not eat the recommended number of grain products.

In Canada, nearly 30 percent of children eat French fries at least twice a week.

Moolicious Milk

From the time you are born, milk is an important source of **vitamins** and nutrients. As babies, most mammals need milk. It gives them the things they need to grow strong. As you grow, your body continues to need milk to be healthy.

In many parts of the world, milk, its products, and milk alternatives are important for humans. Whether you use it on your cereal at breakfast, drink it in a glass at dinner, or snack on one of its products, you likely eat milk many times each day.

Think about your lunch today. Did you have a bowl of yogurt or a slice of cheese? These foods are made using milk. At breakfast, you may have soy milk on your cereal. **Fortified** soy products are milk alternatives.

Types of Milk Products

Cow's Milk

Goat's Milk

Cheese

Soy

Food for Thought

How does white milk compare to chocolate milk and other drinks?

Chocolate milk is white milk with cocoa and sweeteners added. It contains the same vitamins as white milk but has more **calories**.

Milk has ten times the potassium of some sports drinks.

From Cow to Carton

Milk and milk products come from animals, such as cows. To make 1 litre of milk, a cow must drink 2 litres of water. An average cow will make about 90 glasses of milk each day.

Making Milk

1 Dairy cows are the main milk producers in Canada.

2 Most cows are milked twice a day. Milking takes about five minutes.

3 The milk is put inside a large, cold vat. Then, it is sent on a truck to a processing plant.

4 At the plant, milk is **pasteurized** and **homogenized**.

5 Milk is put through more processes so that it stays fresh longer. Then, it is put in cartons and sent to stores.

6 There are many types of milk. Skim milk has all of the **fat** removed. Homogenized milk has no fat removed.

Milk Products

A tall, cold glass of milk is a refreshing way to get the nutrients your body needs, but there are many other great ways to get the same benefits.

Milk, or dairy, products, such as ice cream, cheese, and yogurt, are made from milk and contain many of the same nutrients. Butter, evaporated milk, sour cream, and cream cheese are other examples of milk products.

Food for Thought

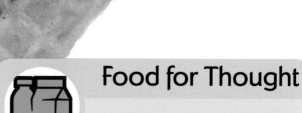

How can you tell which milk products are healthiest?

Not all milk products are created equal. Compare package labels to check the calories, nutrients, and fats found in different products. Look for fewer calories and fats, and more nutrients.

Using yogurt as a fruit dip is a great way to get a serving of milk products.

Get the Facts on Nutrition
Learn how to read a food label

When looking for milk products, it is important to read the ingredient list on the food you are buying. Look at the label on different types of yogurt or cheese to see which offer the most nutrients.

The Nutrition Facts table will include the list of calories and 13 nutrients.

1

2

5

3

4

6

Nutrition Facts
Serving Size 1 Cake (43g)
Servings Per Container 5

Amount Per Serving

Calories 200 Calories from Fat 90

	% Daily Value*
Total Fat 10g	15%
Saturated Fat 5g	25%
Trans Fat 0g	
Cholesterol 0mg	0%
Sodium 100mg	4%
Total Carbohydrate 26g	9%
Dietary Fiber 0g	0%
Sugars 19g	
Protein 1g	

Vitamin A 0%	•	Vitamin C 0%
Calcium 0%	•	Iron 2%

* Percent Daily Values are based on a 2,000 calorie diet. Your daily values may be higher or lower depending on your calorie needs:

		Calories:	2,000	2,500
Total Fat	Less than		65g	80g
Sat. Fat	Less than		20g	25g
Cholesterol	Less than		300mg	300mg
Sodium	Less than		2,400mg	2,400mg
Total Carbohydrate			300g	375g
Dietary Fiber			25g	30g

1 The facts tell you the serving size and the number of servings in the package. The size of the serving determines the number of calories.

2 Calories tell you how much energy you will get from a serving. Children who get at least one hour of exercise each day should eat between 1,700 and 1,800 calories every day.

3 The first nutrients listed are fats. It is important to limit the number of fats you eat each day.

4 The next nutrients listed are fibre, vitamins, and **minerals**. These are the parts of food that keep your body healthy and in great shape.

5 The % Daily Value shows how much of the nutrients you need are in one serving of food.

6 The information at the bottom of the label further explains the calorie, nutrient, and % Daily Value information.

Milk Alternatives

If you are not in the mood for milk or your stomach simply cannot digest it, there are other options. Fortified soy beverages are some of the best choices to satisfy your body's nutritional needs.

Soy milk is made from dry soybeans that have been ground with water. To make soy milk more similar to regular milk, it is fortified. Certain vitamins and calcium are added to give it more nutritional value. Soy milk has about the same amount of **protein** as regular milk, though the types of protein are different.

Some milk alternatives have large amounts of sugar. Be sure to read the label, and pick products that have fewer sugars.

Food for Thought

What are some health problems related to milk and milk products?

About 70 percent of all adults cannot properly digest lactose, a type of sugar found in milk and milk products. Instead, there are low lactose or lactose-free milk products, as well as plant-based milks, such as soy, almond, and oat.

Choosing Milk and Alternatives

Your body needs a certain amount of fats, **carbohydrates**, and protein to keep it powered. It is important to find the right balance. If a person eats 1,800 calories each day, about 203 to 293 grams should come from carbohydrates, 40 to 70 grams from fats, and 60 to 158 grams from protein. This chart shows the calories, carbohydrate, fat, and protein content of some basic foods.

Product	Alternative
Butter 204 calories, 23 grams fat, 0 gram carbohydrates, 0.2 gram protein	**Soy butter** 190 calories, 15 grams fat, 8 grams carbohydrates, 8 grams protein
Ice cream 240 calories, 0 gram fat, 0 gram carbohydrates, 0 gram protein	**Low-fat frozen yogurt** 90 calories, 2 grams fat, 17 grams carbohydrates, 3 grams protein
Process cheese spread 85 calories, 6.2 grams fat, 2.7 grams carbohydrates, 4.6 grams protein	**Hard cheese, parmesan** 111 calories, 7.3 grams fat, 0.9 grams carbohydrates, 10.1 grams protein
Homogenized milk 160 calories, 8 grams fat, 12 grams carbohydrates, 8 grams protein	**Skim milk** 80 calories, 0 gram fat, 12 grams carbohydrates, 8 grams protein

Osteoporosis is caused by a lack in calcium. This disease makes bones brittle so that they break more easily.

Magnificent Milk

Next time you gulp down a glass of refreshing ice cold milk or chomp on a piece of cheese, consider the health benefits. Milk contains nine essential nutrients. They are calcium, riboflavin, phosphorous, niacin, potassium, vitamins A, D, and B12, and protein.

What Is Calcium?
Learn how to keep your teeth and bones strong

Calcium is a necessary part of a healthy diet. It helps keep bones and teeth strong. The human body easily absorbs the calcium found in milk. You would need to eat 1 cup of turnip greens or 2.5 cups of broccoli to get the same amount of calcium that is in two cups of milk.

Children who drink or eat milk, milk products, and milk alternatives often are less likely to break bones or have osteoporosis later in life.

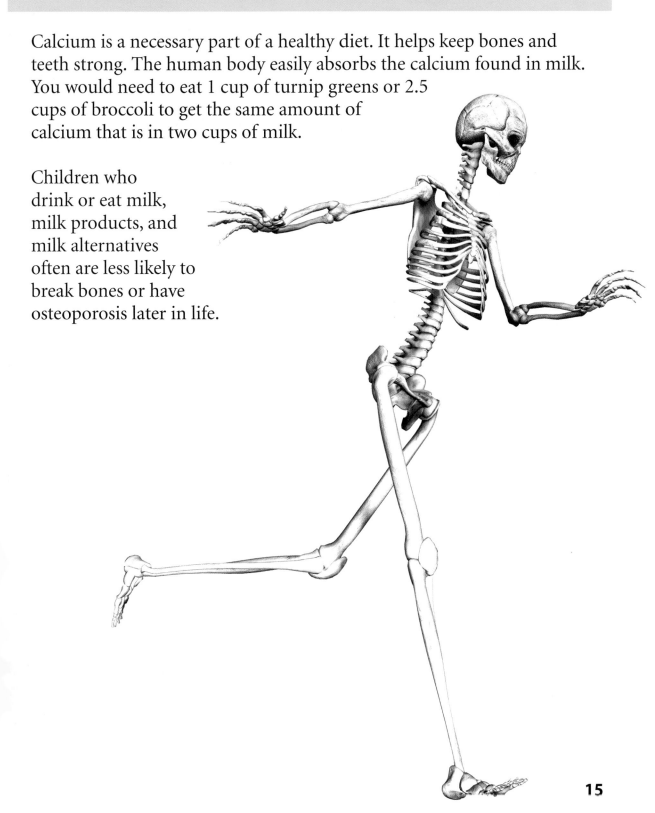

Are You Being Served?

Eating the right foods and enough of them each day will help you get the vitamins and nutrients you need to stay in great shape. Children ages 4 to 13 should have 2 to 4 servings of milk and alternatives daily.

When making soups or casseroles, try using low fat milk or fortified soy milk instead of water.

Try using the foods below to plan a daily serving of milk and alternatives.
Then, mix and match milk and alternative products to prepare your servings for one week.

cereal with 4 ounces of milk

fruit smoothie made with 8 ounces of milk

small container of yogurt (6 ounces)

0.5 cup cottage cheese (equal to 2 ounces of milk)

one slice of hard cheese (equal to 4 ounces of milk)

Counting Servings in a Meal

Check out the servings in a meal with fresh bread, chicken, vegetables, a glass of milk, and an orange for dessert.

250 mL (1 cup) vegetables ➤	**2 Fruit & Vegetables** Food Guide Servings
125 mL chicken breast ➤	**1 Meat & Alternatives** Food Guide Servings
1 slice rye bread ➤	**1 Grain Products** Food Guide Servings
250 mL 1% milk ➤	**1 Milk & Alternatives** Food Guide Servings
1 orange ➤	**1 Fruit & Vegetables** Food Guide Servings

1 cup of frozen yogurt

one scoop of ice cream (equal to 0.33 cup of milk)

1 cup of milk

Tomato soup (1 cup of milk)

1 cup chocolate milk

Fitness Fun

Healthy eating is just part of keeping your body in top form. In Canada, more than 50 percent of boys and 60 percent of girls do not get enough physical activity. From walking to playing team sports or riding a bike, there are many ways to get the physical activity you need each day.

It is recommended that children take part in at least 90 minutes of physical activity each day. This may include playing a sport, walking a dog, or doing yoga.

Food and Fitness Facts

 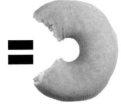

Walking for 22 minutes will burn half of a doughnut.

Thirty minutes of climbing stairs burns a small serving of French fries.

Spending 13 minutes on a bike burns off a glass of pop.

It takes 18 minutes of gardening to burn off 25 peanuts.

WORK ON THIS

If you ate a doughnut, fries, and a pop today, how much would you have to work out to burn off those calories so that you did not gain weight?

Answer: 65 minutes

Calories and Consumption

Your body needs energy to operate. Food provides this energy. A calorie is a unit of energy. Calories are used to measure the amount of potential energy foods have if they are used by your body. A gram of carbohydrates or protein has 4 calories, while a gram of fat contains 9 calories. Your body needs a certain amount of calories each day to function well. If you eat fewer calories than your body requires, you may lose weight. If you eat more calories, you may gain weight. To maintain your weight, you need to burn as many calories as you eat. To burn calories, you need to do physical activity.

Time to Dine

Smart Smoothie

What you will need

0.5 cup fat-free milk
0.5 cup low fat yogurt
0.5 frozen, peeled,
   chopped banana
0.5 cup frozen strawberries

Blender
Glass

What to do

1. Place all of the ingredients in a blender. Blend until smooth.
2. Pour into a glass, and serve.

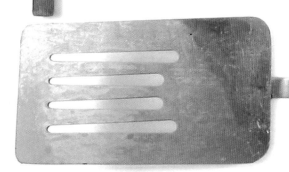

Cheesy Choice

What you will need

four slices whole wheat bread

two slices of your favourite cheese

two slices another type of cheese

1/4 cup shredded crabmeat

two sliced onions

1 tablespoon black pepper

butter

frying pan

spatula

What to do

1. With an adult's help, melt some butter in the frying pan. Then, add the black pepper to the pan.
2. Butter one side of each bread slice.
3. Place one slice of each type of cheese on the dry side of two slices of bread. Then, add a layer of crabmeat and onions. Place one slice of each type of cheese on top.
4. Put another slice of bread on top of the cheese, butter side up.
5. Place the "sandwiches" in the frying pan, and grill. Flip once the first side is golden brown. Repeat on the other side.
6. Let cool, and serve.

What Have You Learned?

What is soy milk made from?

Answer: dry soybeans that have been ground with water

Why is calcium important to health?

Answer: it helps keep bones and teeth strong

How many servings of milk and alternatives should you have each day?

Answer: 2-4

What are the four food groups?

Answer: Fruit and Vegetables Milk and Alternatives Meat and Alternatives Grain Products

What is chocolate milk?

Answer: white milk with cocoa and sweeteners

How can you burn off half of a doughnut?

Answer: walk for 22 minutes

Further Research

How can I find out more about milk and healthy eating?

Most libraries have computers that connect to a database that contains information on books and articles about different subjects. You can input a key word and find material on that person, place, or thing you want to learn more about. The computer will provide you with a list of books in the library that contain information on the subject you searched for. Non-fiction books are arranged numerically, using their call number. Fiction books are organized alphabetically by the author's last name.

Websites

For a copy of Canada's Food Guide, surf to
www.hc-sc.gc.ca/fn-an/food-guide-aliment/index-eng.php.

To learn more about healthy living, download the guide at
www.healthycanadians.gc.ca/pa-ap/cg-cg_e.html.

For information about your body, fitness, food and other health topics, visit
http://kidshealth.org/kid.

Glossary

calories: units of measure for the amount of heat made by a food when it is used by the body

carbohydrates: a compound made of carbon, hydrogen, and oxygen; sugars and starches

diabetes: a disease in which the body has too much blood sugar; treated with insulin, a substance that controls the use of sugar by the body

fat: an oily or greasy substance that is found naturally in animal products

fortified: increased nutritional value

homogenized: a process in which fat, or cream, is dispersed by a machine so that it does not float to the top

minerals: natural substances that are not plants or animals

obesity: very overweight

pasteurized: heated to a specific temperature for a certain amount of time before it is cooled again

protein: a substance that is needed by all living things

vitamins: natural or humanmade substances that keep the body healthy

Index